I0469690

Claim Your Spotlight:
Become an Instant Expert in Your Niche & Walk the Red Carpet to Business Success

CINDY EARL

Cynthia Earl, LLC
Cleveland, Ohio 44140
Cindy@ClaimYourSpotlight.com
www.ClaimYourSpotlight.com

ISBN: 148195945X
ISBN-13: 978-1481959452

Limits of Liability and Disclaimer of Warranty

Warning – Disclaimer

DEDICATION

To my wonderful children, Alexandra and Nathan, who inspire me and make me want to be a better person every day.

To my husband, Tim, this book would not exist without your love, support and all the opportunities you give me to just be me. Thank you for always believing in me.

To my parents, Jane and John, thank you for always telling me I can do anything I want to do, if I believe I can achieve it. Your unconditional love and support give me the courage to go after my dreams.

My friends, you know who you are and I thank you for your unconditional love and support.

To my many mentors and teachers, thank you for sharing your knowledge, guiding me and paving the pathway for me to do what I love.

And to entrepreneurs, solopreneurs and mompreneurs, I dedicate this book to all of you and hope it gives you the courage and resources to do what you love.

Thank you for purchasing this book! Whether you've been in business for years or are just starting out, by following the steps in this book you CAN become the #1 expert, authority and celebrity in your niche.

If you like this book and are craving more content, I invite you to sign-up for my FREE "Spotlight Report" monthly newsletter. It's completely free and contains more tips and strategies, as well as your most frequently asked questions about growing your business. Visit www.ClaimYourSpotlight.com to sign-up today!

If at the end of the book you feel like you have additional questions or you would just like to connect and continue the conversation online, you will find me at:

www.facebook.com/claimyourspotlight

www.linkedin.com/in/cindyearl

www.twitter.com/cindyearl

Enjoy!

Cindy Earl

Founder & CEO

CONTENTS

1 INTRODUCTION

My Story

Everyone has a big turning point at least once in their life.
This is mine…

I was 28 years old and had everything in the world going
for me – two college degrees, a great job I loved, wonderful
family, friends and you just got engaged to my best friend.
It was the happiest time of my life! It's the culmination
of many years of self development, studying and hard work.

One day, while driving to an out-of-town business meeting,
I was suddenly struck with a debilitating dizziness and vertigo.
Strange – I thought maybe it's just a cold or allergies? I
pulled off the highway and decided to get a hotel room to
sleep the night and continue to the appointment in the
morning. I was sure I would be better if I rested.

I had a rather restless night of sleep and the next morning I felt even more dizzy and sick. The room was spinning and I was nauseous. All alone, in the middle of nowhere and I didn't have a clue what's wrong. I was scared. I imagined the worst possible scenarios…what if it's a stroke or brain hemorrhage – something really serious. My heart beat fast, I started to sweat and my anxiety level went through the roof. I felt too dizzy to drive, or even stand up. I needed help. I picked up the phone and called my mom to come pick me up. Life as I know it changes for ever.

What happened over the next 6 months is like something out of a book. The dizziness subsided but I was left with a deep aching soreness in my muscles and debilitating exhaustion. It's like having the flu, but it never went away.

In the medical system, I was shopped around to every doctor and specialist in the book and NO ONE, I mean no one could figure out what was wrong with me. I was tested for every illness under the sun
– EKG, EEG, CT scans, x-rays, cancer screenings, multiple sclerosis, heart problems, pulmonary blood clot, anxiety, depression, Lyme disease, rheumatoid arthritis, muscle testing and more. Every test came back negative. Good news – it didn't appear to be anything life threatening, but I knew something was very wrong. Quitting my job and cancelling the wedding seemed to be inevitable. I could barely get out of bed.

Needless to say, 1997 was a very long and stressful year for me. The following year I finally had a diagnosis – chronic fatigue syndrome and fibromyalgia. Debilitating, but not life threatening. Living with a chronic illness, as you might imagine, changed everything for me.

Despite the bad news, I was grateful to have a diagnosis and began a treatment regiment of medication, exercise and vitamin supplements. Within a few months, I was back to 70-80% of normal function and energy. I was able to have that dream wedding, honeymoon and my husband and I moved into our first new place as a married couple.
But, the illness definitely took a toll on my daily life and still does.

Soon, I realized that continuing to work at my full-time job as a college marketing director was no longer possible. For a career- driven, type-A person like me, this was a devastating blow. I'd had a great career in higher education, but living with a chronic illness deprived me of the energy and strength to keep up with the demands of a fast-paced career.

Enter Entrepreneurism…

In 2001, I took a leap of faith and left my job with plans to start my own freelance marketing/PR business on a part-time basis while working at home so that I could take care of my health and build my career based on my needs. I was so excited that I leapt into my new venture without regard for research, planning, funding or realizing how tough it really is to start a business. I just knew I was good at what I did. For the first several years in business, I really struggled.

I did all the traditional things I thought I should do to market my business – direct mailings, letters, put an ad in the Yellow Pages (a very costly mistake!), advertised in local papers, had expensive full-color brochures printed, etc. Yet, nothing I did was brought in clients.

As I was slowly building my business, I was asked to start a local chapter of a national women's networking organization. Starting this new chapter from the ground-up was quite a challenge, mostly because I had absolutely no marketing budget or funding of any kind. Other people told me I was crazy to accept such a position, but I followed my gut. I knew that running a networking group would get me out in the community in a big way.

It turned out to be one of the best decisions of my life because it opened me up to a new world of possibilities and connections (authors, speakers and business coaches).

I started to implement creative, no-cost marketing methods and within months, my chapter skyrocketed. My monthly networking events sold-out and the number of new members soared. We attracted prominent, six-figure corporate sponsors and multiple media partners. In six months, we were the fastest growing chapter in the nation.

It was so successful I had to turn people away at our events! Even the CEO of the organization, as well as other chapter leaders, started asking me what I was doing to become so successful, so fast. I trained other chapter leaders in my marketing and publicity tactics and they started to see the same success.

And the best part… I didn't spend a dime on advertising.

I loved what I was doing and became very passionate about helping other women to market and promote their businesses. Soon, women started asking me for coaching and advice on how they could use marketing techniques to build their businesses and attract clients. I knew that I had found my calling as a business coach and knew what I had to do.

In 2007, I signed up for a coach training program and became a certified business coach. A year later, I joined a marketing coach training program with a very successful business coach and best-selling author. And no, I couldn't afford it, but I also couldn't afford NOT to do it. I immersed myself in learning from him and the other members of the group.

I also started learning more about online marketing. Facebook and Twitter started to boom and I found that there were much easier ways for me to leverage my time and get the word out about my business in an even bigger way by using the power of social media. I was amazed at the ability of social media to rapidly spread ideas and messages to a much bigger national and global audience than anyone could ever imagine.

Recognizing that social media was the future of marketing, I sought further training (again!). In 2009, became certified as a social media specialist, personally trained by the immensely talented and widely recognized social media guru Mari Smith (marismith.com), I was mentored by Mari and others in the social media industry and it has helped me to help my clients achieve some amazingly positive results.

5

Since then, I've worked with some major business superstars like Kendall Summerhawk, Fabienne Fredrickson, Suzanne Evans, Sandra Yancey, Michael Port and others. I've helped them maximize social media and online marketing to become instant celebrities in their businesses, and I can help you too!

I have always been a marketer and that's what I do, but my unique gift is inspiring women to do big things in the world by helping them tap into their own "Inner Celebrity" (or what I like to call your unique brilliance). I help them become the #1 expert in their niche and leverage that fame to make an even bigger difference in the world.

From the deepest core of my being, this is what inspires, drives, connects and reconfirms my commitment to overcoming my illness and doing the hard work it takes to make a difference and be successful in the world. Beyond money, what really matters to me is impacting women's lives for the greater good.

Why am I Sharing This With You?

Having fibromyalgia is not something I usually talk about. I tell myself I'm tough and fight through the symptoms; acting as if I am 100 percent healthy like the people around me. I'm in denial a lot of the time because I want my body to function as it used to. When I work too much or am too physically active (like planting bushes in my flower beds last weekend – whew!), my body always reminds me through the searing pain that I am not my former self and I'm different from everyone else.

Why am I sharing this with you now? First, I really want to spread awareness of this illness and how it affects 6 million people in the US alone. One whom I admire most is the author Martha Beck (you may have seen her on Oprah or read her bestselling self help books) who has been an inspiration to me as an example of thriving with fibromyalgia. She is not shy about talking about her illness and has a fabulous career as a writer, even thought she suffers with fibromyalgia like I do. Hey, if Martha can do it, then I can too!

It's time to become radically transparent, to tell my story of loss, grieving, pain and suffering, yet ultimately triumphing over this illness. I don't let it keep me down even though there are days that I just can't get out of bed or summon the energy to get through the day. I push through because I want a life with meaning and freedom, and part of that for me is helping others become all that they can be in creating businesses that allow them to live their purpose.

So instead of sharing a story of "woe is me," I'd rather tell you a story of transformation and triumph! For many years I thought that having fibromyalgia was a curse (and some days I still do!), but now I look at it as a blessing/ I've learned so much and really have grown into the person I want to be, despite my physical limitations.

For example, I never would have thought about having my own business before fibromyalgia. Being forced to quit a job I loved as a college administrator was so crushing to me, but I simply couldn't keep up with the pace. I knew I couldn't work full time anymore, but my creative side wanted an outlet. So, 10 years ago I created my first business. I've been on a joyful ride ever since. Now, I can't imagine living any other way. I've been able to build a career around my illness which provides me the freedom to work when I want, where I want, spend more time with my children and family, and have time to rest when I need it most.

Before fibromyalgia, I never really appreciated the little things in life…the stuff that really matters. I recently read an article about the regrets of people on their death beds written by a hospice nurse who found commonality among all dying people. They all had the same regrets. They wished they hadn't worked so hard or spent more time with friends. They wished they had spent more time with the important people in their lives instead of working for the corporate machine. I do not want to have those regrets! That's exactly what pushes me to live my purpose though my work.

Each one of us was put here for a reason and despite illness, loss and limitations; each of us has the power to create the life we want.
Choose happiness over sadness. Find out what we love to do and create and income out of it. Live life to the fullest and fulfill your purpose, no matter how hard life is sometimes. In her last show, Oprah said something that really stuck with me, "You alone are enough. Each one of us was put on this earth for a reason. Your job is to go find your purpose and live it."

Although still a work in progress, I strive every day to live my

purpose to help others build businesses that fulfill their purpose and feed their soul. You alone are enough! You have gifts to share and you have a choice to live a happy life. Having a happy life really is
a choice. It took me a long time to realize that. I choose to live my purpose through my business. I'm doing the work I was meant to do.

How about you? Do you consciously see the lesson in every thing that happens in your life, or do you blame others for your unhappiness? Are you living your true purpose, or are you grinding it out, day by day in a job you hate. You have a purpose to live, are you seeking to find it, or accepting your life the way it is and settling for being less than happy?

You have to power to turn it around. There is a lesson in everything – you just need to find it. I've learned so many lesions from having this illness that I almost can't imagine not having it. Is your burden to bear a blessing or a curse? Choose blessing and the Universe will reward you with more than you ever imagined.

Big Shifts in Marketing

We are at a crossroads in history where everything we know about marketing and communication is changing rapidly. Whether you realize it or not, we are right in the center of this movement. You must adapt to marketing in a social media world.

Marketing and PR have changed dramatically. We are living in a world constantly bombarded by media (and consumer opinion which has quickly surpassed traditional media as a source of credible, reliable information). Consumer opinion and rating is often given even more consideration than third- party media in making purchasing decisions.

Take Amazon.com for example: whose advice do you trust most when reading a review for a book – the book critic in the newspaper or the reader rating on Amazon? The consumer has more influence than ever in the marketplace.

Having said all of this, however, after being so immersed in social media over the past few years I realized that it is only one piece of the marketing pie. These days, with so many marketing channels, you have to create a digital and offline footprint across multiple marketing channels. Not only that, but standing apart from your competitors is more challenging than ever. There is so much "noise" out there, how do you as a small business owner or entrepreneur stand out from the maddening crowd of people who do what you do?

The answer is within you…and you probably don't even know it.

If you are reading this book, you probably:

- Have a message you want to share with the world
- Love what you do but you're not so good with the marketing stuff
- Dream of delivering your message, product or service to thousands of people with incredible authority and credibility.
- Want to be recognized for your knowledge and talents, and also be paid what you are worth

If this sounds like you, I know what you're craving, what you're about and where you'd like to go. What's more, I also know what's standing in your way.

My guess is you have a burning desire to contribute, to make a difference, to help people. You're an entrepreneur, a small business owner, consultant, coach or service provider. You're great at what you do, but you are trading time for dollars – and there are only so many hours in the day. You know that there is more to life, you want more clients, more income but you also want to know how to expand your reach without spending more hours.

You want to get paid for your knowledge. You know there is so much potential in today's marketplace, but you don't know how to capitalize on it. You want leverage, freedom, control and financial independence. I'm so glad you are reading this book! You are about to embark on an amazing journey and I hope this book will motivate you along your path. You absolutely can do what you love AND make money.

2 TAP INTO YOUR INNER CELEBRITY

Life is a live performance with you in the lead role.

You can take the play of your life in any direction you choose.

– Ansleigh McCloud

Every person is born with a unique brilliance – a God-given gift that is unique to only you. Some people (like actress Meryl Streep or musician Sheryl Crow, for example) know it at an early age and for others it takes a lifetime to discover. It really is one's life quest – to find your unique brilliance and share it with the world.

If you haven't yet discovered your unique brilliance, don't worry. It is deep within you, you only need to find the best way to tap into it. I refer to it as your "Inner Celebrity" because I believe we can all be a star in our own right. Discovering this essence is the really the first key to a successful, happy, fulfilled business and life.

Each one of us is unique. Look at yourself and identify how you differ from others. What is special about you and your product or service that make you stand out from the crowd? Then come up with fresh, innovative ways to tell the world about you.

If you are just starting out or have been in business for while and are feeling like you just aren't connecting with people or are discouraged by the lack of clients and customers, first take a good look at your strengths and passions.

Many people jump into business without this important foundational piece and end up miserable and unsuccessful because they lose passion and interest in what they are doing. But, you can avoid a passion-less business venture if you start with a few simple tips.

First, have a crystal-clear vision of exactly what you want. Think seriously about your needs and desires in terms of your personal &

professional relationships, money, freedom, work & home environment, and spirituality. If you have a clear vision in writing, it is harder to let that vision go or let the dream die.

Second, share your gifts. Your life experience has value and people are meant to be transformed by your connection and your talent.
Care enough to keep going. Care enough for others to share and keep going. I had one business coach who called this "share your brownies." If you make great brownies, share them with people who love brownies!

If you're not exactly sure what your unique gifts are - no worries. For most people, this takes some time to discover. Over the years, I've tried many ways to discover this brilliance within myself. I've read tons of self-help books, attended countless seminars, and literally have spent thousands of dollars on my quest. Maybe you can relate? As a result of all my years of study, I've discovered several of the best ways to help you tap into and uncover your "Inner Celebrity." I'd like to share a few with you here.

Mind Mapping

I love mind-mapping! It's the best way to organize ideas. You can do this exercise on paper by drawing a circle in the middle of a piece of paper and labeling in the center of the circle "What I Know" or "What I Love." Each thought you have on this topic is written as a "spoke" that comes from the center circle. If you are a visual person like me, this is an easy way to see your thoughts on paper.

You can also use mind-mapping software called Mindjet (mindjet.com) for a small fee. Mindjet allows you to do this exercise neatly right on your computer and save the files for future reference. I have used both methods and both are equally effective.

Once you have your center circle, begin to think about everything you know. And I mean EVERYTHING! Don't censor yourself, just do a complete brain dump of everything that comes to mind.

Once you have everything dumped, and written down on paper, take a look at your list and choose the top two or three that you are most passionate about. Take those ideas and break them down even further by creating separate mind maps for each. You will now have three mind maps.

Visualization

This is a technique I learned from one of my very first coaches. It's amazingly powerful and may bring you to tears, but I think you'll get a lot out of it. Here is the exercise:

Sit in a quiet place. Close your eyes and reflect. Don't be afraid to let your emotions out, as that's when you will know for sure you are on the right track.

As you are sitting quietly by yourself, imagine a room full of all the people who you love and care about and who have been your biggest cheerleaders. These can be family members, teachers, clergy, mentors, bosses, colleagues, friends, and anyone else you can think of   in your personal network.

Now, imagine you walk into the room, right down the center, through the crowd and you can see each and every face as you walk by. They are all here to celebrate you and your life. As you take the stage and turn to look at the crowd, gaze upon each face, one-at-a- time. What are they saying about you? Remember, these are the people who respect and adore you. You have touched their lives in some profound way and they are here to celebrate YOU.

Next, write down every thought that comes to your mind (if you can write through the teary eyes!). When you finish writing   you   should have a long list of your best qualities, unique abilities and your core brilliance. Look at how they all relate to each other. You will likely see a trend. Write down that trend in one statement, for example:

"Cindy is a great inspiration, she is a great organizer, she cares deeply for people and has the unique ability to tap into a problem and come up with a quick, creative solution in no time. She is very perceptive and intuitive."

Do you see how this relates to what I do in my business every day? Now, what's yours?

Self Assessment

Self assessment is tricky. We are usually completely unaware of what makes us different or unique. This is why in addition to self

17

assessment I suggest you also survey your friends, family and clients too. To identify your unique qualities and characteristics, first disregard all of your preconceived ideas. Try to be completely unfiltered with your thoughts when you do this exercise. Most of the time, our pre-conceived notions are completely false.

For a quick and easy self-assessment, complete the following personal checklist:

Name

Age

Place of

birth

Family

Spouse

Children

Parents

Siblings

Other

family

Education

Occupation

Previous careers

How and why did you start your business?

Interests, hobbies

Special skills

Awards or accomplishments

Then, ask yourself these key questions:

What do I love?

What am I best at?

What could I do all day and lose track of time?

What do I care about deeply?

What change to I want to see in the world?

What do I stand for (think big, global terms)?

After you complete your own personal checklist, now go ask your close friends and colleagues for their feedback. You are likely to get answers you never would have expected and great insight into how others perceive you.

Here are some example questions to ask your friends and colleagues:

What are my best qualities?

What three words would you use to describe me?

What do you think is my biggest talent?

What do you think I'm best at?

How do you see me?

What do you think I love the most?

What do you think my values are?

Next, compare your lists and start to see the patterns and connections that appear. Which of the ideas jump out as opportunities to create an income for you that incorporates your passion, skills and interests? The sweet spot for your business is the crossover between what you love to do and what people will pay for.

Example:

Let's look at Samantha. Samantha was a successful real estate agent who grew tired of working long hours and spending weekends away from her family. She knew she wanted to work from home so she could spend more time with her children. Samantha began searching the Internet for a viable solution to working from home. Like many of you, she found several opportunities and even tried some out.

Nothing quite took off like she hoped and she spent a good deal of money trying out several failed ventures. Then she began to think about what really drives her and motivates her.

After completing the self-assessment exercises, she wondered if she could transfer her love of real estate into something that she could do from home. She thought about the resources she already had available to her as well as the years of experience she had selling real estate. She had proven sales skills, a natural ability to communicate with clients and customers, knowledge of the real estate market, several contacts in the real estate training business and great computer skills.

Her "A-Ha" moment occurred when she asked herself, "What would a new real estate agent need to know to be successful?" Then she found her starting point for creating income doing what she loved, but in a different way. She discovered that she could transfer her knowledge into products and services those other real estate agents or agents-in-training would be willing to buy! She turned her knowledge into an e-book first, and then developed written training manuals and an online membership website with video tutorials.

This is a simple example of how a person could take their passion, skills and interests and turn it into a viable form of income. Using this example, what can you come up with for yourself?

Books

If you still aren't 100% sure what your specific skill set and talents I recommend checking out some of these books (book descriptions from Amazon.com):

Unique Ability: Creating the Life You Want by Catherine Nomura, Julia Waller, and Shannon Waller – "You have inside you an incredible force called Unique Ability. It's a combination of your personal talents, passions, and skills. You've always had this ability, but you may never have stopped to clearly identify it. Few people do. When you begin to figure out this important foundation of who you are, you'll understand what you do best in life, what you love doing most, and what makes the most difference for the most people. You'll also be able to focus on doing more of what works in your life and stay away from what doesn't work. This book offers a simple and powerful approach to creating a life that works, a life that you love, because it comes from who you truly are and what you're all about. This book contains a complete process that will help you identify your Unique Ability, then immediately put it to work in your life."

Strengths Finder 2.0 by Tom Rath – "Do you have the opportunity to do what you do best every day? Chances are you don't. All too often our natural talents go untapped. From the cradle to the cubicle, we devote more time to fixing our shortcomings than to developing our strengths. To help people uncover their talents, Gallup introduced the first version of its online assessment, StrengthsFinder, in 2001 which ignited a global conversation and helped millions to discover their top five talents.

In this latest national bestseller, StrengthsFinder 2.0, Gallup unveils the new and improved version of its popular assessment, language of 34 themes, and much more (see below for details). While you can read this book in one sitting, you'll use it as a reference for

decades. Loaded with hundreds of strategies for applying your strengths, this new book and accompanying website will change the way you look at yourself--and the world around you--forever."

Finding Your Own North Star: Claiming the Life You Were Meant to Live by Martha Beck – "Martha Beck has helped hundreds of clients find their own North Star, fulfill their potential, and live more joyfully

Now, she shares her step-by-step program that will help you take the exhilarating and frightening journey to your own ideal life. Finding Your Own North Star will teach you how to read your internal compasses, articulate your core desires, identify and repair the unconscious beliefs that may be blocking your progress, nurture your intuition, and cultivate your dreams from the first magical flicker of an idea through the planning and implementation of a more satisfying life. Martha Beck offers thoroughly tested case studies, questionnaires, exercises, and her own trademark wit and wisdom to guide you every step of the way."

The Four-Hour Workweek by Timothy Ferris – "Forget the old concept of retirement and the rest of the deferred-life plan– there is no need   to wait and every reason not to, especially in unpredictable economic times. Whether your dream is escaping the rat race, experiencing high-end world travel, earning a monthly five-figure income with zero management, or just living more and working less, The 4-Hour Workweek is the blueprint."

Do What You Love and The Money Will Follow: Discovering Your Right Livelihood by Marsha Sinetaur – "You're about to be liberated! Here is   the book you've been waiting for-a-step-by-step guide to finding the "work" that expresses and fulfills your needs, talents, and passions.
Using dozens of real-life examples, Marsha Sinetar shows you how to overcome your fears, take the little risks that make big risks possible, and become a person whose work means self-expression,   growth, and love!"

The Artists Way by Julia Cameron – "With the basic principle that creative expression is the natural direction of life, Julia Cameron leads you through a comprehensive twelve-week program to recover your creativity from a variety of blocks, including limiting beliefs, fear, self-sabotage, jealousy, guilt, addictions, and other inhibiting forces, replacing them with confidence and productivity."

DiSC® Assessment (www.discprofile.com) – "DiSC® is the leading personal assessment tool used by more than 40 million people to improve work productivity, teamwork and communication. DiSC® is a personal assessment tool used to improve work productivity, teamwork and communication. DiSC® is non-judgmental and helps people discuss their behavioral differences."

Kolbe Assessment (www.kolbe.com) – "The Kolbe A Index measures a person's instinctive method of operation (MO), and identifies the ways he or she will be most productive. It need only be taken once, since these innate abilities do not change over time."

Spend some real time on this. Don't skip over it. Discovering your unique brilliance and natural ability is the key to finding a real foundation for your business and to creating a great hook that captures the attention of your ideal clients, prospects and the interest of the media.

Intuition
Don't forget to listen to your gut. Let your intuition guide you to the right path. Your intuition is speaking to you all the time. You just

need to learn how to tune in and listen. One of the best ways to do this is through meditation.

I know meditation is not for everyone. As entrepreneurs our minds are going a million miles a minute all the time with ideas and it's very hard to sit still. But I have found the more you practice the better you get. Find a quiet place and start out with 5 minutes. You can begin by simply asking a question (to the Universe or God or whomever you think of as your higher power) and quietly listening to the answers that come.

For example, you might start by asking "What is my highest and best use on the planet?" or "How can I serve others?" The answers may come as thoughts, feelings, smells, images, or something you read or hear. You might not get the message right away, but pay attention to what happens in your every day life after you pose these questions.
The answers will come in unexpected places. It's all possible, you just have to believe in your gut that it is.

Finally, remember just because you CAN do something, doesn't mean that you should. Simply having a skill doesn't mean you have a passion for it. Don't fall into this trap like I did starting out. Just because something comes easy to you doesn't necessarily mean that you should make it your life's work.

Real success in business only comes when you match your skills (your strengths and abilities) with your passion (what drives you). Passion alone will not sustain a business. You also must have an audience who need your knowledge and are willing to pay for it.

Your passion (you may also hear this referred to as your "why") helps you make a BIG difference in the world. It's what motivates you to get out of bed every day to do what you do. Doing something you love and are passionately motivated by the first step to a creating successful business venture.

3 YOUR STAR QUALITY

Stories are the creative conversion of life itself into a more powerful,
clearer, more meaningful experience.

- Robert McKee

Mindset

To be successful in business I've learned that skill and ability alone are not enough. You also must be sure your mindset is in the right place. Henry Ford once said, "If you think you can or you think you can't, you are right." In other words, if you think you will fail, you will fail. If you think you will succeed, you will succeed. Having a success mindset is equally, if not more important, than your talent.

Having a strong "why" is critical to your mindset. When things get rough and you find yourself tempted to run away or quit (because it will happen, guaranteed), remember to that you always have your "why" to fall back on. Your "why" is the purpose that drives you and the reason you get out of bed every day to do what you do. Have confidence and know that you can do it! If you feel compelled to share your message, it is because there is a ready-made audience out there ready and willing to hear it.

The fact is many of us still have a really hard time promoting ourselves without feeling as if we are bragging. Why is this? As girls, were never taught how to boast about ourselves. We play in a cooperative manner and are more concerned with inclusion, relationships and how everyone in a group is getting along rather than about winning or losing. While this is an incredibly valuable skill and women are known to be better relationship builders, we often do ourselves a disservice when trying to compete in a world where both sexes are competing.

Note that women are starting businesses at twice the rate of men, yet no more than 10% ever hit the $1 million mark. I believe big part of the reason for these statistics is that many women simply lack the confidence to ask for what they need. Ladies, the first step to confidence building is as simple as learning to like you.

Jennifer Read Hawthorne, co-author of Chicken Soup for the Woman's Soul, believes that learning to like and even love oneself is a lifelong process. "You can surround yourself with competent leaders, but you can never really compensate for low self-esteem. Sooner or later, you will be discovered." Hawthorne recommends several tactics for boosting self-esteem:

1. Make sure your business is your passion. Your low self-esteem could be tied to not following your heart.

2. Associate with people who seem genuinely happy. Happy people are usually at peace with themselves.

3. Ask for help. Don't try to work on your issues alone.

I agree it's important for women to pursue their passions and also believe women need to manage their expectations. The perspective that "only perfection is good enough" limits our advancement in both business and life. Once we accept that perfection is not the norm, we can have the freedom to take risks, make mistakes, and pursue our dreams. Learning to take "imperfect action" will propel our businesses forward.

Your "Behind the Music" Back-Story

Do you remember a show on the cable channel VH1 a few years back called "Behind the Music?" It was a documentary-type show which told the back-story of a musician or band that had once been famous, but had fallen out of the limelight. It was always about how they got famous, experienced an inevitable fall from grace via drugs, addiction or over exposure, and then discovered a road back to newfound peace. They were always such great stories – you were literally glued to the TV and had to watch.

Just like "Behind the Music" stories, you must have your own personal narrative (hopefully without the drugs and addiction!). It's the story of whatever has happened in your life, good or bad, which fuels your passion in business and quickly builds the "know, like and trust factor" with your ideal clients and prospects. This is a story that they can relate to quickly because they see some of themselves in it.

If you come from an authentic place, your success is almost guaranteed. Your story is what will set you apart from the crowd. Write your unique, compelling story using the following questions as a guide.

Here are a few questions to get you started:

1. What has happened in your life, good or bad, that would be most useful to share with other people?

2. How did you get to where you are today?

3. What event(s) caused you to be on the path you are on?

4. What reason(s) do you do what you do (or what you want to do)?

Here are a few examples of a strong back story:

- A woman who started a graphic design business because she wants to save money to pay for her children to attend college.

- A business consultant who wants to make a difference in his community by helping small businesses become profitable and contributes to the economic development of the region.

- A mother of a child with autism who wants to share what she's learned about autism with other parents so they can live better lives.

Your back story incorporates your WHY – knowing what's behind the passion about your area of expertise. It encompasses your expertise, your big vision and creates a relationship with your ideal prospects based on credibility and trust. Building trust takes time. Don't expect it to happen overnight just because you put up a website.

Your Brand

Many small business owners don't put enough time into thinking about their brand. To start building a powerful brand platform, you have to become the number one, go-to expert in your niche.

Contrary to popular belief, your logo is not your brand – neither is your tagline. Your brand is about how you want to be seen in the world. So, ask yourself these questions:

- "What is the core message I want to share with the world?"

- "What would I like to be known for?"

- "What do I stand for?"

I have re-branded my business several times over the years. Many people have asked me – why did you change your brand and how did you do it? The main reason I chose to make over my brand is that I got to a point where I was no longer inspired or excited about my business. It got so bad that I nearly QUIT. Have you ever felt that way? Maybe it's time you look at re-branding.

So many of you are spinning your wheels with marketing, but don't feel like you're getting any traction. Or you spent a lot of money on a fancy new website, with lots of bells and whistles, but still aren't getting any new clients.

I'm here to tell you, if you don't have a strong brand platform and a strong WHY, your marketing will never work. In order for a marketing strategy to be successful, you've got to have a solid brand foundation.

Here are the three main things you need to know about branding.

Be Authentic

> First and foremost, your brand must be authentic. It must authentically represent the core of your personality and uniqueness. Before delving into re-branding, take a very close look at who you are inside. What makes you tick? Try asking yourself these important questions:
>
> - What makes you get out of bed everyday to do what you do?
> - What qualities do others admire in you?
> - What ticks you off (this is a clue to the innermost reasons you do what you do)?
> - What experiences have you had in your lifetime (good or bad) that have shaped who you are? You may have heard the line "make your mess your message." Often our life experiences are what fuel a passion within us to change the world.
> - What difference do you want to see in the world?

For many people, the prospect of sharing your authentic self publicly can be a little scary. Believe me you are not alone. Most business owners I know (including myself) struggle with getting personal in their business. However, this is the most powerful way to create a deep connection with your audience. Your authenticity is what people relate to and it's what lets them know you are the one for them – because they see themselves in your story. Coming from a place of real authenticity is what will attract your ideal client to you effortlessly. It literally pulls them to you.

Clarify Your Message

You've got to get crystal clear about your WHO, WHAT, WHY and HOW. If you aren't clear about who you are, your target market, what you offer and the value you provide, how can you expect your ideal client to be clear about you, and most importantly, buy from you?

Focus your messaging on the results that you get for your clients, not just the benefits or features of your product or service. People gather information through benefits, but they buy results. Think about results in terms of Financial, Emotional, Physical or Spiritual gain (I use the acronym FEPS to remember this). What are the deep underlying reasons that people need to do business with you? What problem do you solve for them?

A good example of this is one of my clients named Debbie who is a dog massage therapist (I know – pretty cool right?). Before our work together she was very focused on the benefits to the dogs she worked on, which included things like pain relief, greater mobility and better health. But when we looked deeper, and I asked her "What are the results for the dog owner?" things started to click. Obviously, it is the dog owner that is buying and paying for her services – not the dog!

Once she realized that her real clients are the dog owners, we came up with a brilliant tagline for her business: "Comfort for your dog. Peace of mind for you." This statement not only addresses the benefits for the dog, but the deeply rooted result for the pet owner – peace of mind that they are doing everything possible to help their dogs live a pain-free, active life. The result for the dog was physical (the P in FEPS), but the result for the dog owner was really emotional (the E in FEPS). Do you see what a big difference this makes?

Your Logo is Not Your Brand

Many entrepreneurs make the mistake of thinking that a brand is just a logo. Your logo and your website, along with other visual components, such as advertising, business cards, Facebook pages, Twitter backgrounds, speaker kits, client gifts and more, contribute to the development of your brand. They are not, however, your brand.

They are merely visual associations that create a brand in the mind of your target audience. For example, if you want to be thought of
as organized, systematic and direct, then all of the visual components

of your brand must express this in some way in order to affect the words, images, thoughts and feelings that come up in the mind of your target client. Successful branding clearly communicates your brand attributes (those authentic questions you asked yourself earlier), so that when someone sees the visual elements of your brand, those qualities shine through.

One of the most brilliant ways I've seen successful business owners craft a unique brand is by creating their own "Spotlight Name."

4 YOUR SPOTLIGHT NAME

"Be who you are and say what you feel, because those who mind
don't matter and those who matter don't mind."

- Dr. Seuss

After you've spent some time and have a better sense of your unique brilliance and your brand, it's time to get creative! It's great to know what you are brilliant at, but then you have to get out there and prove it to others and put yourself on the map!

One of the best ways to do this is by creating what I call your Spotlight Name. This seemingly simple technique is commonly used by the most successful business owners I know.

Why It Works

A Spotlight Name is your own personal headline. It's a short, concise way of describing yourself and your unique brilliance in one quick snippet. It's what makes you instantly recognizable from all the other people who do what you do. It's a unique "hook" to hang your entire business on and a shortcut to explaining what it is you do.

Your Spotlight Name is the name you want to get known by, stand out and get noticed for what you do. It's the thing that makes you instantly recognizable and communicates your unique brilliance to the world. With a Spotlight Name, your marketing becomes so easy, sales become effortless and competition is virtually eliminated.

To further explain, let me give you some examples (some are more familiar than others!):

- The Smile Doctor
- The King of Pop
- The Queen of Soul
- The Ezine Queen
- The Shopping Cart Queen
- The Tech Coach
- Dr. Brand
- The Booger Doctor (pediatric allergist)
- The Wine Coach
- The Barefoot Contessa
- America's Doctor
- The Property Brothers

A Spotlight Name is a very tangible, super quick to communicate and represents your entire brand. It has to be a short, easy-to-remember, savvy name that says exactly what you do and gets you noticed (and is easy enough for a 5 year old to understand). Do you see how this name can become the hook that all your marketing stems from?

Don't be too clever. You must be taken seriously. If you can take out your name and replace with your competitors, it's not enough. This can only be YOU. The Spotlight Name makes you stand out from the crowd of business owners that do what you do to attract your ideal client.

The Spotlight Name is actually a micro-version of your story. It gets your personality across, while describing who you are, what makes you special and why your ideal client should take notice. It should compel your ideal client to ask you for more information. Your ideal client reaction when they hear your name should be: "I need to talk to her! I found the person to solve my problem, move me forward...that sounds interesting. I want to find out more."

Your Spotlight Name makes it easier for ideal client to choose you. With so much noise in marketing, it helps your ideal client easily identify that you are someone they need to speak to. Essentially, it does your marketing for you!

Your Spotlight Name precedes your networking introduction, elevator speech or what I call your "Spotlight Introduction" (which we will cover in the next chapter). Remember, this doesn't have to be perfect and it may not be the same forever – people evolve. Simply pick the one that works for you right now. Done is better than perfect!

Create Your Own Spotlight Name

Here are the simple steps to creating your Spotlight Name:

1. Clearly state what you DO – what is the transformation you offer – what are the results I make happen (not what you do). List all the words, phrases, and expressions that describe this (remember to think about FEPS).

2. What's different about you?
   Think of words, phrases and expressions that are a little out of the ordinary that describe your unique ability and what you do.

3. What sets you apart and positions you in your market? What is the relationship you have with your audience? Where are you in it? Use words, phrases and roles that describe the market position you want to claim.

4. Who is your target audience? Let people know they are in the right place. Clearly state exactly who you work with.

5. Share your personality.
   Choose words and phrases that describe you, who you are, and what you are like.

6. Finally, add all these words together to come up with some descriptive 'headlines.' See how they words work together.

Play around and have fun with this! This should be a fun,

creative exercise. If it helps, write the words on index cards   so you can lay them out and mix up the words to come up with different combinations.

Also, don't be afraid to stake your claim! As I tell my clients, once you stick your stake in the sand, define your Spotlight Name and share it with the world, the prospects and clients   will start rolling in. It is the universal law of attraction at work! (If you're not familiar with the law of attraction, run   out and buy the book "The Secret" and read it right now!).

5 YOUR SPOTLIGHT INTRODUCTION

"People will forget what you said, people will forget what you did,
but people will never forget how you made them feel."

- Maya Angelou

Explaining who you are and what you do in a way that will generate an emotional connection, interest and action from your target audience is the first step in self-promotion. However, it is often the most overlooked aspects of marketing your business. Clearly articulating what you do so that your prospects understand it immediately is challenging and takes time to prepare.

Before you start promoting your business to the world through social media or any other marketing channels, make sure you prepare by first being clear about who you are, what you do and why you do it. Take some time to brainstorm some of the problems your clients encounter and what you do to solve them.

How to Create Your Spotlight Introduction

One of my biggest pet-peeves about networking events (you know the ones where you go around the room and everybody shares their elevator speech) is the sheer lack of originality and passion in people's pitches. If you can't sound passionate, articulate and genuinely excited about what you do, how do you expect your prospects to get excited about working with you?

Clearly articulating what you do so that the prospect 'gets it' immediately is challenging and takes time to prepare. As you are out and about networking, attending events and meet-ups, think about incorporating some of the following tips into your conversations.

Remember, if you are in business, you are always networking! You

45

never know when or where the right connections can happen! You need to be prepared at all times. You never know when you might run into the perfect client at the grocery store.

To start crafting your introduction, first determine who and what your audience wants or needs. You should understand the needs or "pain points" of your prospect before making an introduction.

Potential customers don't really care that much about you or your business. They just want to know how you can help them. People want quick, painless, easy solutions to their problems, needs and desires. Make that connection for them and you are in business!

Use this simple formula to craft your Spotlight Introduction:

I help_____(your target audience)

who_____(the pain point/problem you solve)

to_____(your solution)

so that_____(the #1 result you deliver for your clients).

For example:

I'm Cindy Earl with ClaimYourSpotlight.com. I help small business owners who want to grow their business to get known online, attract more clients and make more money!

Another way to phrase this is:

I teach_____(your solution)

to_____(your target audience)

even if_____(their pain point).

For example:

I teach online marketing to small business owners and entrepreneurs even if they know nothing about marketing or technology.

You get the idea! Now craft your own Spotlight Introduction. Make sure you focus on the real, concrete results you achieve with your clients, rather thank simply the benefits and you will be amazed at the response.

Now that you have your introduction ready, it's time to get out there and network (both offline and online)! Here are a few of my best networking tips to enhance your experience and results.

- Incorporate the prospect's name in one-on-one introductions. You want to show your prospect that you paid attention to their name and that it matters to you. Remember, the sweetest sound to anyone is the sound of their own name.

- Be focused and clear. All of your focus and attention is on the prospect no matter how many people are in the room or standing by.

- Within the introduction your prospect should hear something that clearly indicates what you offer could be a benefit to her. Engage your prospect by sharing your expertise, knowledge and an irresistible free offer.

- Create a reason for someone to share the news about you and what you offer. You want others to view you as a priority contact, not only for themselves, but for others.

- Be flexible! One size does not fit all! Adapt your language to the individual you are speaking to or circumstance you are in.

- Look for opportunities to open doors for others! Successful people make things happen for others. They provide access to people and resources.

- Remember that most purchasing decisions are emotionally based. Create a vivid mental picture for your prospect and how their pain is relieved by your solution.

- Ask questions and be a good listener. By asking good questions, you can adapt your conversation to fit the other person's needs.

- Practice! It's ok to write your introduction down, take it with you to events and practice on different audiences. You should have several introductions prepared to use in any situation.

- Adapt this Spotlight Introduction as your description in your social network profiles and other online communities. This will create consistency in your message across all platforms.

So the next time you're at a networking event or someone asks you, "What do you do?" please don't give a standard, boring and bland statement like, "I'm a lawyer" or "I'm a business coach." Be creative and remember that we are all in business to solve our client's problems. Remember, your Spotlight Introduction is just about starting a conversation. Make it interesting!

6 YOUR CELEBRITY PLATFORM

"Marketers need to build digital relationships and reputation before closing a sale."

- Chris Brogan

While social media is the hottest marketing trend right now, we cannot forget that social media is only one piece of the marketing equation. To achieve business building and income generating results, you must have an integrated approach to marketing. I am a big fan of social media for marketing small businesses, but having taught social media marketing to many groups and after consulting many clients over the past few years, I am convinced that it cannot be your only marketing strategy.

You-Everywhere

In today's "Googling" world, you must take a multi-channel approach to marketing and promoting your business. You need to reach your prospects in the way(s) they like to communicate and where they already gather. These hang-outs can be online (ex: on a blog) or offline (ex: at a business association meeting). Ask yourself these questions:

- Do they prefer email, or text?

- What blogs or publications do they read?

- Where do they network?

- What groups are they members of (both online and offline)?

- What social networks do they prefer?

Luckily, in our modern information age it's easier than ever to find out this type of information. Social networks offer the opportunity for instant market research. You need only to do a few searches on Google to find out where your prospects are. I cannot stress enough that you cannot market yourself online with a website alone. You need to build a multi-channel online footprint.

To give you a good example of what I mean, look at recording artist Taylor Swift. For instance, you can find Taylor in multiple places online. Not only does she have TaylorSwift.com as her stand-alone website, she is also present in many of the other places her fans hang out online. She has a Facebook fan page, a Twitter profile, a YouTube channel and a MySpace profile. Her music is available on iTunes, Amazon.com, and major retailers like Target. Her merchandise includes t-shirts to lipstick to Hallmark cards and everything in-between.

She also has mega-promotion deals with companies like Papa John's pizza, where you can event purchase her new CD and have it delivered to your door with your pizza. Talk about expanding your brand!

Of course, I know that you don't have the money or resources to market yourself like Taylor. I am sure she has a huge marketing team behind her, but you can take some clues from her example.

So, how do you expand your online footprint to be in more places where your target audience hangs out?

The Spotlight Marketing Strategy

53

The marketing model that I have learned over year of study and working with many clients and mentors is what I call the Spotlight Marketing Strategy. It includes a multi-channel marketing system that makes sure you and your business are positioned as the #1 expert and authority in your niche.

Online Marketing Channels

According to a Forrester Research Study (Sept. 2012), 84% of small and midsize businesses are using online marketing tactics, but perceptions about the effectiveness vary. Only 25% said that online marketing was a game changer that allowed them to compete more broadly. This is likely because many of them don't know how to market online effectively.

Overall engagement with social media is much lower (roughly 48%) for small to midsize businesses compared with 66% of their larger enterprise counterparts. Small businesses can take a lesson from larger brands who are actively engaged in social media marketing and seeing positive results in terms of lead generation, involvement and customer service.

Businesses in competitive markets or categories would benefit from developing an online marketing plan and getting established alongside larger enterprises. For most businesses, the formula for success starts with visibility and traffic.

People need to hear about a business or product or see its name somewhere multiple times before they make a purchase. In advertising, it used to be commonly accepted that a prospect needed to see your ad (called 'impressions') seven times before they would take action. However, in today's overcrowded information age, that number has jumped to 10-20 impressions!

Online, this is accomplished when a business appears all over the Internet in the places their prospects and clients frequent most (i.e. in search engines, directories, and social networks) where prospective customers look for information, the business type, product or service. Yet, it's not enough to simply appear in these online places, but be active and engage prospects through relevant and compelling content and relationship building. This is where prospects can engage with companies in "conversations" that eventually lead to business relationships.

Proactive businesses are making plans to get these prospects to follow them, friend them, subscribe to their channels, etc. Once connected, businesses start offering information, recommendations, news, coupons, etc. in an effort to get prospects to give permission to follow up with them using whichever methods they prefer (email, mobile, phone). These businesses are building relationships with prospects, earning their trust and ultimately earning their business.

Once a business establishes relationships with prospects online, they need to continue to provide valuable information and continue to make offers. It is proven that it's six to seven times easier to get an existing customer to buy from you again than it is to get a new customer to buy from you the first time.

Most businesses miss opportunities to incrementally increase their income because they don't follow up with their customers. The problem is that most small to midsize business owners find it difficult to allocate their time and/or money to develop an online marketing program.

The Big "Ah-Ha"

At the very core, every business wants and needs to build their brand, save money and increase sales.

The two biggest challenges are:

- Marketing and promotion of the business

- Generating new contacts, leads and referrals

How you meet those challenges depends on your marketing and promotion. That's why you need the proven "Spotlight Marketing Strategy."

Whether you've just launched your business or you've been in business for years, you are going to need a clear, step-by-step plan that you can follow every single day for more clients, customers and cash flow–starting right away.

I believe that if you follow this system, consistently, over time you will finally enjoy not only more credibility and visibility as a celebrity in your niche, but more referrals, more raving FANS, and more consistent income than ever before.

Now you know the WHY in your business – the next step is defining the HOW....

The "HOW"

So, what is the Spotlight Marketing Strategy? It consists of seven different strategies, which combined create a powerful marketing and promotion machine for your business.

Spotlight Strategy #1 – Strike a Pose Online with Your Own Blog Website

Think of your blog as the center of your social branding wheel. It's your social home base. You can be out utilizing all of the social media tools and platforms in the world, but if you don't have anywhere to send your friends and followers to outside of those platforms, your efforts will be in vain.

You may already have a website and that's great. However, a traditional website is static, meaning it doesn't change much. Occasionally you may update the information, but for the most part it functions as a pretty "brochure" for your business. I highly recommend a blog-site, which is a combination website and blog. Wordpress is by far the best of the blogging platforms available.

With the WordPress platform, if you don't want to wait for (or pay for!) a Webmaster to make changes and adjustments to your site, you don't have to. WordPress makes it easy for anyone to administer his or her own site without needing heavy technical knowledge.

Think it all might be too time-consuming or complicated? Think again, because it's actually pretty simple. If you can edit a Word document, you can create your own blog/website.

Spotlight Strategy #2 – Grow Your List, Boost Traffic
and Create Your Automated Follow-Up System
Online, much of your job centers on driving traffic to
your website or blog so that prospective clients or
customers can find out more. One of the best ways to
increase the chances that someone will eventually buy from
you is to build an email list.

Social media is an easy and cost-effective way to drive
traffic and build your list, but it is only one way. Using sites
like Twitter, Facebook, LinkedIn and YouTube along with the
other strategies list-building will maximize your results for
more traffic, more subscribers, more clients and more sales.

Spotlight Strategy #3 – Become a Social Media
Celebrity As a small business owner, it's important to
your success to understand social media's benefits and why
it's worth the time to
learn and make a part of your marketing routine. It's also easy to feel
overwhelmed and not know where to begin or what to do on
each of the different networks.

It doesn't have to be that way — you just need to figure
out WHERE to specifically focus your efforts, and use some
simple but effective methods to clarify your strategy, hone
in on your personal and professional brand. By identifying
your most ideal connections,

you know exactly where to spend your time and the type of content to share with them.

Spotlight Strategy #4 – Create and Launch Your Own Celebrity Info Products

Working one-on-one with clients can be very rewarding as well as lucrative. However, for solo professionals, it can also be exhausting…and sometimes frustrating as well. This is because they are often only focused on selling services or products at the highest price point they offer.

If this sounds familiar, you may adore your clients and love helping them, but are feeling burnt out or stuck because one-on-one sessions are all you are offering. So what's the solution?

Leveraging your time and talent by diversifying the ways you earn income in your business. One of the greatest things about running all or part of your business online is how EASY it is to do this. (Let's be honest, it's no fun when a few of your clients all quit in the same month and you're left scrambling to replace that income.)

Similarly, if you are finding prospects saying they can't afford what you offer, you still don't want to lose them completely. They've shown interest in you already–wouldn't it be great to still be able to help them at a price they are willing to pay?

Some marketers refer to this as the "funnel" or "pyramid" system of marketing and it is really quite clever. Because not only does it allow you to still be able to make a sale, if you've provided value at that lower price point, customers are more likely to come back and buy from you repeatedly—and at higher prices.

Having multiple streams of income is considered leveraged because it is all about reaching more people—without spending more of your time. It's brilliant! You too can do this by packaging your knowledge into products and programs that you can sell for additional income.

Spotlight Strategy #5 – Leverage the Media with Power PR

One thing is for sure, getting your business noticed in the media immediately builds credibility and your business quickly gains momentum. Your business grows and you have more business than you ever dreamed of. It's so fast and dependable, it's practically on autopilot.

Do you know now why?

- PR never sleeps. It is a 24/7 process. It represents YOUR business to tons of potential new clients, even when you're not there

- PR makes you stand out. It puts you in the driver's seat as the expert in your field.

- PR is the center of EVERY marketing campaign. If no one knows who you are and what you do, sales don't happen and new clients don't hire you.

- PR is an underestimated secret weapon and it's practically FREE.

You can get FREE publicity for your business – quickly, easily and consistently, even if you know nothing about PR. You just need to learn a few simple public relations techniques. You can create your own successful PR campaigns to build your brand and attract loads of new clients.

For example, one of my clients sent out her first online press release to increase the number of sign-ups for a free webinar she was presenting. Within just a few days of distributing the press release through PRWeb.com, her registrations increased by nearly 50%, and the press release received over 6,200 reads (or hits) online via Google, Yahoo and other search and news websites. No other traffic building technique can produce the same highly targeted traffic so quickly for pennies per click.

Spotlight Strategy #6 – Network Like a Celebrity
Most people cringe at the thought of networking. It feels unnatural, uncomfortable and scary for most people, especially women. We are not programmed naturally to self-promote.

However, it is a skill that can be learned and is absolutely critical to your business success. What I've found is that the combination of social networking and face-to-face interaction can be very powerful. Social networking on Facebook, Twitter or Linked In can dramatically accelerate the relationship development in between face- to-face meetings. You still need to get out there and meet people – see and be seen.

Step #7 - ACTION! Putting Together Your Spotlight Marketing System

Last but not least, every successful business owner has a documented marketing system they follow, year-in and year-out, to grow your business beyond your wildest dreams.

Beginning with completing the steps in this book to tap into your inner celebrity, set up your strong brand platform and clear messaging, you will have a great platform to start with. Then by implementing the Spotlight Marketing System, you will work the plan and then rinse and repeat. There is truly no limit to the growth–and income–you can achieve.

Following this system positions you as the #1 expert or celebrity in your niche. If you are seen as an expert, people will be willing to pay more for your expertise. This often takes price out of the equation when attracting new customers and clients.

The thing is everything you need to become an instant celebrity in your niche is inside you right now. With the right strategies, tools and coaching you have the ability to tap into your inner celebrity and shine.

7 CONCLUSION

"You already have the ability necessary for success.

- Zig Ziglar

As I mentioned in the Introduction to this book, my first career was in higher education. I actually started out as a college career counselor (i.e. coach!) at several universities. The reason I was drawn to career counseling was due to my own struggle to find out what I wanted to do with my life during my freshman year in college. I was kind of a geek (okay, I was a total geek!) and spent a lot of time in the career center at my school doing lots of personal assessment and research on different careers that matched my personality and skills.

One of the first books I read during this time is called "Do What You Love and The Money Will Follow" by Marsha Sinetaur. It greatly influenced me and has kind of become my life philosophy ever since.

Many of my college friends thought I was nuts for spending so much time on my career research. They just simply chose a major and stuck with it...never really giving a whole lot of thought to what they were really passionate about.

It's those same friends who now find themselves in jobs they hate and lives that are without passion. They're simply going through the motions of life and are either too stuck in their rut or too scared to investigate other options. Nothing frustrates me more than seeing brilliant, capable people who aren't living up to their full potential and suffering a less than satisfying life because of it.

I want more for my life, don't you? I want to be passionate about what I do and jump up every day feeling excited about work. I want to know that I make a difference and help other people. Fortunately, I do! I'm a "Passionista" and you can be too.

My experience in career counseling taught me a lot. I learned that every person is gifted with a unique ability. I know that it's our job on the planet to find out what our ability is and to share it with the world in a big way.

The best way I've found is through entrepreneurship. Being in business for over the past 10 years has been the journey of a lifetime. I've grown in ways I never could have imagined and in the process, have helped others grow as well. Nothing could be more fulfilling to me.

If you want to stretch yourself to live full-out and do what you love – being an entrepreneur is absolutely the right path for you. I would love to help you along your entrepreneurial journey and get out into the world in a really big way. In fact, it's what I absolutely love to do.

You see, in addition to knowing a lot about career development and self assessment, I'm also an expert at helping you identify, package and market your unique skills and abilities to the world. I've been doing it for myself and others for over 15 years now, and I know I can help you. Not only help you, but significantly reduce your learning curve and put you on the fast track to success.

You don't have to put in a decade of learning like I did to get you where you want to go. I've done the legwork for you and know what it takes to be successful – I've been there, done that and here's what I know for sure:

- Marketing is not cookie-cutter. You have to make it authentically you

- You have to get comfortable stepping outside your box   and being totally honest and real with yourself and your prospects

- You'll never be successful trying to replicate someone else's business (I know because I've tried it and spent a lot of money in the process)

- If you feel you have a message inside of you that's screaming   to get out, it's because there is an audience of people ready to hear it

- You cannot do this alone

You have unique gifts to share with the world. Isn't it time the world knew about you?

Think about it...What if you could actually do this? What would your   life look like if you were able to build your income by sharing what   you love with the world? Think about all the people out there who desperately need your help.

I can guarantee, if you have a message to share, there is an audience ready and waiting to hear it. When you think about it this way, it's really your obligation to share your message. Don't hold back your gifts. Whatever your vision, you can make it happen with some effort and the right tools and mentors.

CLAIM YOUR SPOTLIGHT

Get out there and build your

platform. It's your time to shine in

the spotlight!

8 WHAT'S NEXT

If you liked this book and are craving more content, I invite you to sign-up for my FREE "Spotlight Report" monthly newsletter. It's completely free and contains more tips and strategies, as well as your most frequently asked questions about building your business. Visit www.ClaimYourSpotlight.com to sign-up today!

By following the steps in this book, you will have a strong platform to build upon. What if there was a marketing system that you could use to fill in the blanks, simplify the process and shave years off your learning curve so you can maximize online marketing to produce profit, boost credibility and build your business? There is.

It's called the Spotlight Marketing Home Study System. It is a proven, do-it-yourself, step-by-step system that ANY entrepreneur or small business owner can use to attract more clients online and create a joyful, authentic and rewarding business!

In the Spotlight Marketing Home Study System, I'll personally walk you through the nuts and bolts of how to design and run a business that leverages your unique ability and the power of the Internet to build a profitable business. You'll get everything you need to implement what you learn quickly, including instructional videos, checklists, scripts, templates and more.

Whether you've been in business for years or are just starting out, you CAN implement this entire step-by-step marketing system to become the expert, authority and celebrity in your niche.

For more information, visit www.ClaimYourSpotlight.com.

CINDY EARL

9 WHAT PEOPLE ARE SAYING

"Before working with Cindy, I was confused by social media and didn't have a strategic plan to make the best of it. Our social media strategy was more hit or miss rather than consistent. Therefore we weren't fully utilizing it to build our business.

Cindy taught me how to take consistent and deliberate action to implement our social media strategy. Now I know how to fully utilize social media and I also understand which pieces of social media can be undertaken by my team (to allow me time to focus on my business) and which areas I needed to focus on myself. As a result of working with Cindy, we have been able to grow our business using social media and have seen many new clients purchase our products and programs as a direct result of social media activity.

Cindy has a very clear action plan which lays out exactly what you should be doing when. She shows you which activities you need to focus on daily and weekly so that you can make the best use of your social networking time. And she lays it out with clear worksheets and templates.

Suzanne Evans

SuzanneEvans.org

"Before working with Cindy, I knew I needed some help implementing my social networking plan but was having trouble finding the right person. I knew social networking was important for the bottom line of my business so I needed someone who understood how it fit into my overall marketing strategy. Cindy has helped tremendously. In just a few short months of hiring Cindy, my following on Twitter increased by 200% and I added well over 1,000 fans to my Facebook fan page.

Those results along with all of the other marketing pieces I have in place in my business allowed me to sell out my high-end "Money, Marketing and Soul Intensive Workshop" in record time. I was even able to track several paid workshop participants who found me directly through social networks.

Plus, I've greatly increased my visibility and created a greater presence in those spaces. If you are looking for someone who really knows social media marketing, I highly recommend Cindy."

Kendall Summerhawk
KendallSummerhawk.com

"Cindy Earl is committed to empowering women entrepreneurs to build successful businesses and make positive contributions in the world (and have fun doing it!). I am so confident in Cindy's ability that I recommended her social media expertise in my best-selling "Book Yourself Solid, Second Edition.""

Michael Port
NY Times Best-Selling Author of Book Yourself Solid, Beyond Booked

Solid, The Contrarian Effect & Think Big Manifesto
BookYourselfSolid.com

"Cindy founded the Cleveland chapter of eWomenNetwork in 2002. Within the first year, it was one of the top chapters in North America due to Cindy's energy, passion and creativity. She was the first Managing Director to bring on paid sponsors for her chapter. We were so impressed with Cindy's ability and knowledge that we asked her to help develop our chapter sponsor program and national corporate sponsorships for eWomenNetwork. Because of Cindy, we were able to bring on a major bank sponsor, plus several other high- profile partners. I highly recommend Cindy as a coach, marketing professional and advocate for women's business."

Sandra Yancey, Founder & CEO
eWomenNetwork.com

"Before working with Cindy I was really lost with regards to the direction I wanted to take with social media. I knew I needed to get involved but did not have a plan and that is where Cindy really helped me with my business. While working together, the process of creating my social media strategy became clear and I knew what I wanted to do and what Cindy was going to do to help me along the way.

As a result of working with Cindy, I now have a clear path and I am aggressively working the plan. I have grown my LinkedIn, Facebook, and Twitter contacts and presence 10x where I was before I started working with Cindy. I now have a social media presence and we are working currently to launch my first book.

My advice for those thinking of getting Cindy's social media marketing system or coaching with Cindy is to just know that she will do a great job and her follow through and ongoing help is great.

Cindy is also a super nice person and a pleasure to deal with."

Doug Hecker
2ExcelNow.com

"Before working with Cindy I felt a bit lost in the world of social media. I know I needed to be leveraging Facebook, Twitter and LinkedIn but was not sure how to create a cohesive social media plan.

Cindy's Social Media Bootcamp was amazing! She walked us through each of the most important elements of a comprehensive social media program and showed us how to maintain this in 20 minutes a day. I have cut the time I spend managing my social media program in half but have continued to increase my followers/friends. If you are considering working with Cindy I only have one question: "What are you waiting for?"

Laurie Forster
TheWineCoach.com

"Cindy helped me to finally implement my social media strategy/communication plan after several years of trying to make it happen on my own. I couldn't have done it without her guidance, education and support. My investment has been returned tenfold and   I receive frequent positive feedback on my content since Cindy assists me in getting it distributed on a consistent basis. "

Jeanne Coughlin
CGroupinc.com

"I am thankful for Cindy's social media guidance. The Social Media Marketing Plan that she designed for me this past year has
really helped me "get out there" in a really BIG way! Increased visibility, stronger connection to my "Circle of Friends/Fans"…resulting in a boost to the Bottom line as my private   personal training and coaching practice stays consistently full!"

Jeff Brandes
JeffBrandes.com

"Thank you for being on my team. Your marketing abilities are awesome and as a result of working with you, I have achieved great success. My first international speaking assignment was   related   to your contacts. I am booked solid with 11 speaking jobs this month. Thank you, Thank you!"

DeLores Pressley
DeLoresPressley.com

"I have participated in Cindy's training sessions and webinars. She   has a knack for coming up with creative ideas to help women business owners market and expand their business. She has a common sense approach and a lot of patience when it comes to explaining what type of social media marketing works best for your business. I learned more about using Facebook in a 15 minute conversation with Cindy than I had in countless other discussions. If you're wondering how to build your business, I would highly recommend Cindy!"

Jackie Swanson

justamomentimages.com

"Cindy's attention to detail and positive attitude make her an asset to any organization. Her commitment to helping small business grow is evident in all activities. Her passion for public relations and project management are two of her greatest capabilities. I would highly recommend Cindy."

Neen James
Neenjames.com

"I have a deep respect for what Cindy contributes to people. She is passionate about helping business owners communicate, set and meet their goals and make a positive contribution in the world. I highly recommend Cindy for marketing consulting, copywriting, business consulting and inspiration."

Leslie Curruthers
TheSearchGuru.com

ABOUT THE AUTHOR

CINDY EARL, M.Ed. is Founder & CEO of
ClaimYourSpotlight.com. She is a Registered Corporate Coach
(RCC) certified Book Yourself Solid® Marketing Coach & social
media specialist. Through ClaimYourSpotlight.com, she helps
entrepreneurs grow their businesses using authentic relationship
marketing & simple, proven marketing strategies.

Her products & services simplify marketing for thousands of small
business owners, authors, experts, speakers, coaches and consultants
worldwide. She is a graduate of Ohio University with a B.S. in
Organizational Communication and a M.Ed. in Higher Education
Administration.

Cindy lives in northeast Ohio near Cleveland with her husband and
two children. You can learn more about Cindy and her courses,
programs and products at her website
www.ClaimYourSpotlight.com.

www.ingramcontent.com/pod-product-compliance
Lightning Source LLC
Chambersburg PA
CBHW071247170526
45165CB00003B/1271